HIMALAYAN PILGRIMAGE

HIMALAYAN

A Studio Book · The Viking Press · New York

ERNST HAAS

PILGRIMAGE

Text by Gisela Minke

Acknowledgments

For much valuable assistance during my travels in the Himalaya and during
this book's preparation, I am particularly indebted to: The Government of
India, The Royal Government of Bhutan, The Royal Government of Nepal,
His Holiness the Dalai Lama, His Holiness Gyalwa Karmapa, His Holiness
Kaushak Bakula, The Venerable Jamgon Khongtrul Rinpoche, The Venerable
Tepo Rinpoche, Lama Lobsang of Ladakh Buddha Vihara, Tenzin Geyche,
Mrs. Pema Gyalpo, His Excellency Lyonpo Sangye Penjor, Mrs. Rinchen
Dolma Taring, Mr. Jigme Taring, Mrs. Tess Dorji, Mr. Lobsang Lhalungpa,
Mr. Rinchen Sadutshang, Dr. Phuntsok of Leh, Major General R. T. Morlin,
AVSM, Mr. Salim Rizvey, Mr. Akhbar Ladakhi, Mr. Tashi Rabgay, Mr. Bryan
Holme, and Mrs. Marina Filicori.

First published in 1978 by The Viking Press
625 Madison Avenue, New York, N.Y. 10022
Published simultaneously in Canada by
Penguin Books Canada Limited

Library of Congress Cataloging in Publication Data
Haas, Ernst, 1921–
   Himalayan pilgrimage.
   (A Studio book)
   1. Himalaya region—Description and travel.
   2. Lamaism.   3. Temples, Buddhist—Himalaya region.
I. Minke, Gisela.   II. Title.
DS485.H6H24   954   78-17677
ISBN 0-670-37237-4

Printed and bound in Switzerland by Roto-Sadag
Set in Garamond

Contents

Photo Notes

Neither my equipment nor my technique has changed very much in the past ten years, during which I traveled extensively in the Himalayan region to make the photographs for this book. Although I occasionally use the handy Leica M4 camera (with 35-mm and 50-mm lenses) for fast and flexible situations, I now photograph almost exclusively with the new Leicaflex system. Its dependability in any kind of extreme weather—which I encountered often in the Himalaya—is extraordinary. I always use Kodachrome film 25 and 64 and Leicaflex lenses of 21, 28, 35, 50, 90, 135, and 180 mm. What I love most about these lenses is their sharp, clear definition, and the result is never too harsh, as sharpness alone is not enough. With the exception of a polarization filter, which I find ideal for reducing reflections and glare, no other filter was used during my work on this book. In order to travel as lightly as I can, the rest of my equipment is kept to a minimum: a little Leica table tripod, which I use when longer exposures are necessary, and a small handle, which I use when I need to get a firmer grip.

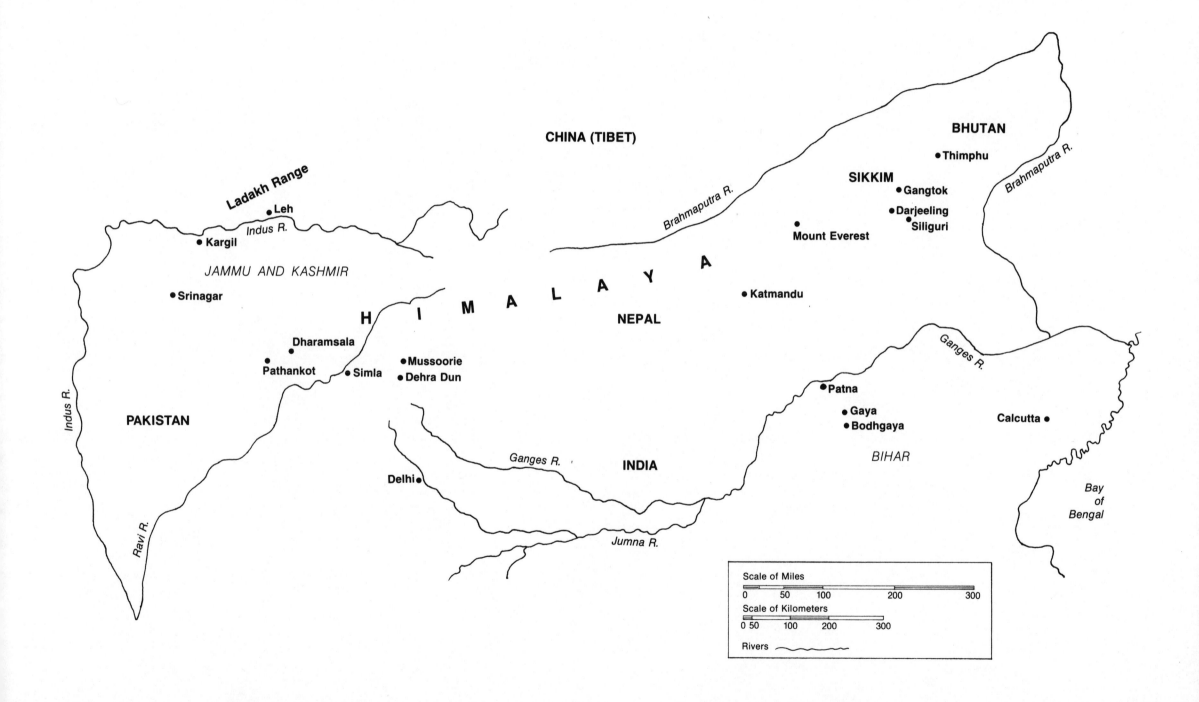

CHINA (TIBET)

BHUTAN
● Thimphu

Ladakh Range
● Leh

SIKKIM
● Gangtok
● Darjeeling
Siliguri

Indus R.
● Kargil

Brahmaputra R.

Brahmaputra R.

● Mount Everest

JAMMU AND KASHMIR

H I M A L A Y A

● Srinagar

● Katmandu

NEPAL

Dharamsala

Ganges R.

● Mussoorie

Pathankot ● Simla
● Dehra Dun

● Patna

Indus R.

PAKISTAN

● Gaya
● Bodhgaya

Calcutta ●

BIHAR

Ganges R.

INDIA

Bay
of
Bengal

Delhi ●

Ravi R.

Jumna R.

Scale of Miles

0   50   100   200   300

Scale of Kilometers

0 50   100   200   300

Rivers

Introduction

Mountains have always meant a great deal to me. I grew up in Austria, and I am grateful for the things that mountains have taught me — awareness, endurance, and discipline, all of which are so important in life.

My interest in exploring the Himalaya was therefore motivated not only by geography and my profession as a photographer but also by a fact that had long intrigued me: that the highest mountains in the world seemed to have inspired the highest levels of the human spirit.

Even during my initial visit to the Himalaya I found myself becoming less and less interested in climbing the highest peaks, and more and more interested in absorbing the wisdom of the people who lived at the top of the world. Symbolic of this dual sensation of height, the external and the internal, is the photograph on the jacket of this book, which shows the Lamas to be even higher than the mountains.

My first visit to the Himalaya occurred in 1968 during a six-week photographic tour of India at the invitation of the Government of India. The last week of this assignment found me in Darjeeling, and it was there that I first met Tibetans. In 1959 thousands of these brave people had fled their native land to find political refuge just across the border.

Because of Tibet's isolation from the rest of the world, I had expected the Tibetans to be quaint, or at least strange, and because they had fled from their native soil, I was also prepared to find them bitter, sullen, and withdrawn. They weren't that way at all. Like so many Westerners before me, I was surprised and totally captivated by them. They seemed so unspoiled, so unpolluted by the mechanical world. They radiated such deep faith, dignity, tolerance, and gentleness and displayed such a delicious sense of humor that for me it was love at first sight.

The Tibetans would seem to have mastered their national tragedy much better than we in the West have managed to do at various times in our history.

I grew up in Vienna, a city close to a border where, in 1956, minefields and watchtowers failed to hold back hundreds and thousands of Hungarians and, little more than ten years later, the many thousands of Czechs who fled their homeland after their sad short spring. If there is a country which has compassion for the plight of refugees, I would say it is Austria. During the war and postwar years Austria was deeply committed to giving shelter, hope, and a new life to people who believed in a different definition of freedom from the one forced upon them. But although the Austrians and other nations in the West managed to rebuild their material world after two terrible wars, they have never really regained their spiritual balance. The search for spiritual values has spread from Europe and has now become almost universal.

I soon learned that the great inner strength of Tibetans is rooted in their unique form of Mahayana Buddhism, and I longed to learn about it. Thus began a personal pilgrimage to the many places in the Himalaya where the culture of Tibetan Buddhism still flourishes.

Although I was educated toward a rational, scientific way of thinking, I never really believed in its absolute truth; it always seemed to me that something was missing. The philosophy and wisdom of ancient Tibet confirmed my instinctive belief and refined it. Sounds, colors, movements, gestures, all the senses, I realized, were interrelated and could be aroused and directed in a certain way toward a higher level of consciousness. Having been preoccupied all my life with the visual world, I felt an immediate affinity with the Tibetan ways of visualization and meditation.

My own idea of the visual image goes far beyond that of the spoken or written word. Without meaning to belittle the power of the word, its poetic implications or scientific significance, I do believe that even in this so-called visual age the beauty and strength of the purely visual dimension are still sadly neglected.

One of the troubles with visual-minded people like myself is that while they are photographing, they tend to become almost deaf and dumb or, one might say, lost in a sort of visual meditation. This is by way of admitting that to accomplish my mission in the Himalaya — the longest and most important in my career — and to produce this book within any reasonable length of time would have been impossible alone. I was fortunate to find in my friend Gisela Minke a partner who kept notes and wrote down names, who secured official permission to travel where travel was not normally permitted, who arranged for food and shelter in many out-of-the-way places, who secured transportation, and, above all, who was able to describe in the chapters that follow the experiences and impressions gained during our travels in the Himalaya. Perhaps this is the right place to say thank you to her for arranging the many details that a busy photographer is apt to take too much for granted.

Besides showing the magnificence of the Himalaya, its colorful people and their customs, the majority of the photographs in this book are portrayals of feelings. In attempting this, I came to appreciate many of the expressions coined by the generation of the last decade, expressions such as "high," "far out," "out of sight," all of which grew out of drug-related experiences. The deep longings of the postwar and Vietnam War society reached out for spiritual values which more often than not deteriorated into artificial means of escape and, in turn, enslavement. While drugs can induce illusions, never do they

truly enlighten. On the other hand, through the practice of Tibetan Buddhism and other ancient religions and through meditation, an increasing number of people in search of truth are currently traveling along much safer paths.

I am certainly no expert in esoteric matters, but seven years of exploring the Himalaya and living with the people in that fabulous part of the world has been an experience never to be forgotten. And I am not the only one to have fallen under this spell. Thousands upon thousands of people, especially young people, from the industrialized West, after coming to the high mountains, have returned to their homelands not only awed by the scenery but inspired by the message of the Dharma. I doubt that the spiritual influence of any region has been greater or more lasting than that of the Himalaya. To try to define all the reasons would only show that we have not understood its wisdom. One thing I learned long ago is that if you cannot answer your own question, you should go back and question your question.

What has happened in the short space of a decade is phenomenal. I remember that ten years ago, if I ever spoke of meditation, mandala, Lama, hardly a soul knew what I meant, while today words like these are becoming part of our everyday vocabulary. As new centers and meeting places keep springing up all over Europe and America, it would seem safe to say that more people have become interested in Mahayana Buddhism than in Maoism, although the latter tried so hard to extinguish all traces of the Mahayana tradition in Tibet proper.

I am aware of the dangers of overromanticism. Suddenly to be transplanted into an unmechanized world where people live as they lived centuries ago has a profound effect on one. Yet I rarely felt like a stranger among them. And the more I grew to understand the strength of their faith the more I realized the good influence it was having on others. It was at once evident that living simply need not be the result of poverty or ignorance but of wisdom. Similarly I learned the importance of giving and receiving gracefully, of shying away from the fanatical, and striving for a deeper understanding of nature and a compassion for all sentient beings.

There are many excellent books on Tibetan religion and philosophy available. I am not a scholar or a writer, but a photographer, and I feel a little like the Tibetan at the Kalachakra Initiation who was questioned by a Western student about the deeper meaning of certain rituals and symbols. Slightly amused, he answered, "I am only a Tibetan, not a Tibetologist."

E.H.

Mussoorie and Dharamsala

A Tibetan Legacy

The Himalaya is different things to different people. To Indians, it is the "abode of snow," mystical home of the gods, source of all their great and sacred rivers. To the rest of the world, it is the "roof of the world," where the towering peaks have always attracted adventurers and mountain climbers.

Our own image of the Himalaya had been formed in childhood through the books of Sven Hedin and Alexandra David-Neill, Marco Pallis and Heinrich Harrer. Theirs was the Himalaya of the Tibetans and Tibetan culture, the Buddhist Himalaya. For years Ernst Haas and I had both longed to visit Tibet, the "forbidden country" of which those early travelers had written so glowingly. By the time the journey became possible, the Tibet of old had vanished. A cruel fate had closed its doors more tightly than ever, but not before some hundred thousand Tibetans had managed to slip out, following their beloved leader, the Dalai Lama, into exile in India and other neighboring countries.

This exodus—one of the most tragic and least talked about of modern times—had one happy result: it afforded the outside world its first close contact with a great civilization and an ancient and esoteric form of Mahayana Buddhism. The time of the Tibetans' arrival in India coincided with a period in the West when many young people, disillusioned with an increasingly scientific, materialistic way of life, had begun to search for new—or rather old—values. Traveling in the East, they looked for sources, and many found them in India proper or in the Himalaya.

Ernst Haas and I did not come to India as seekers, but during our long travels in the Himalaya we found new insights and values that were to change our lives. It is difficult to express in words some of our deeper experiences. The photographs will speak more eloquently. This text is meant only as a general guide to our intermittent seven-year journey through most of the Buddhist regions of the Himalaya.

When the first Tibetan refugees arrived in India in 1959, worn out by the long trek across the huge mountain barrier, their health breaking from exhaustion and change of climate, they realized the cool air of the Himalayan foothills was preferable by far to the blistering heat and dust of the plains. A sympathetic Indian Government tried to find shelter for them in those mountain regions, thus starting the first transit or refugee camps in Kalimpong and Darjeeling, Simla and Mussoorie, Dharamsala and Dalhousie. Not by accident these very places had once been summer retreats for another group of foreigners from colder lands. During the nineteenth century the British had established these hill stations all along the southern ridges of the Himalaya as family resorts and school towns. Darjeeling and Simla had once even been summer capitals for the colonialists and had taken on a completely British look, with Christian churches, boys' schools modeled after Eton, and summer homes with such names as "Windamere" and "Woodstock Cottage." After India won its independence in 1947, the hill stations lost their *raison d'être,* and the relics of a British past fell into disrepair. Then came the Tibetans, who strung up prayer flags, built

Buddhist shrines, and provided a whole new cultural infusion.

Out of the first primitive refugee camps and self-help centers grew permanent Tibetan settlements where the exiles now try to preserve some of their unique culture and artistic tradition. It is a small leftover of a once-rich heritage, but one that is nevertheless deeply moving.

Our first lengthy stay in the Himalaya coincided with the Buddhist New Year and the prayer festival of Mönlam, when all Tibetan settlements bustle with activity. Driving north from Delhi on a clear wintery day in 1971, we arrived only a few hours later in Mussoorie. This pretty little town is perched on a ridge several thousand feet above the Gangetic Plains and enjoys a particularly pleasant climate. From its colorful bazaar we had a spectacular view south over the fertile Dun Valley and north toward the snow-covered Gangotri peaks and the more distant ranges along the Tibetan border. A short walk down into the next valley took us to what used to be the fashionable West Side of Mussoorie and which our Garwali *kulis* called "lama bazaar." It is the site of Happy Valley, a Tibetan settlement built around a Central Tibetan

School, an orphanage for several hundred children, an old people's home, and a small temple. A truly enchanting place, it was in due time to become like a second home to us.

On this first visit we were received by the legendary Mrs. Rinchen Dolma Taring, an aristocrat from Lhasa, who in 1960 had gathered the first motley group of orphaned and desperately sick children into The Tibetan Homes Foundation and has been the secretary and soul of this model project ever since. She took us around the valley with its three dozen gaily painted houses, all donated by Indian and international relief agencies, and told us of the incredible hardships and difficulties she had encountered over the years. Little of the suffering is visible today. Instead one sees hundreds of rosy-cheeked, happy youngsters in dirndl-like Tibetan national dress romping around or doing household chores. They are divided into groups of about twenty-five, and each group has its own house with two dormitories, a kitchen, and a lovingly decorated prayer room which doubles as dining room. House parents try to give the children the best possible substitute for a normal home.

During the week we spent with them we shared their simple meals and watched them decorate the altars, print new prayer flags, churn butter for the little butter lamps, and prepare special pastries for the approaching Buddhist New Year. Buddhism completely permeates everything in this little Tibetan enclave, much as it did in Tibet. To watch Mrs. Taring and her husband, Jigme, deal with the many practical and emotional problems of their charges was to see Buddhist teachings put into action. We came to admire greatly not only their compassion and patience but the Tibetan way of life in general, and we felt a desire to visit more refugee settlements. The Tarings urged us to go to Dharamsala in the neighboring state of Himachal Pradesh, the residence-in-exile of the Dalai Lama and thus the focal point of Tibetan life.

The night train carried us to Pathankot. From there we went by bus through the beautiful Kangra Valley. Dharamsala consists of several loosely connected communities on the southern slopes of the Dhauladhur range. Climbing slowly to the topmost village, McLeod Ganj, we passed the only reminder of its days as a popular British hill station: the little Christian church of St.-John-in-the-Wilderness where one of the British viceroys lies buried beneath tall Himalayan deodars.

One never has to search long for Tibetan settlements. Prayer flags fluttering in the wind and rock carvings bearing the sacred syllables *Om Mani Padme Hum* are sure to lead one to another "lama bazaar." McLeod Ganj centers around the hilltop compound of the Dalai Lama's temple and residence. In Lhasa the Kyabgon Rinpoche, the Precious Protector, lived in exalted isolation in the Potala, one of the most magnificent structures ever built. Now his home is a modest bungalow surrounded by trees and flowers and guarded around the clock by Indian police. The setting is unpretentious, but to Tibetans the site of His Holiness's residence is always sacred. They immediately started another Lingkor like the one in Lhasa, a circular path around the Dalai Lama's residence. There pilgrims make endless rounds, murmuring, *"Om Mani Padme Hum,"* as they spin their prayer wheels. Some of the older generation circle the mountaintop by throwing themselves on the ground again and again, to cover the whole length of the way with their bodies.

Approximately two thousand refugees live in the lit-

tle village and the surrounding forests, some still in the traditional Tibetan yak-hair tents. It was the eve of Losar, the Tibetan New Year, and we followed festive crowds to an open square near the temple where the first of many rituals was to take place. Huge straw effigies were erected, laced with firecrackers and then set afire. Like youngsters everywhere, the Tibetan children shrieked with excitement and joy. After this *Kehraus* of the old year, things became much more solemn. The rising of the new moon during the following night signaled the arrival of the iron/hog-year, and good fortunes had to be invoked with long prayers and symbolic offerings. All night we could hear the chanting of the monks in the temple.

When a gloriously sunny spring morning rose over the mountain peaks, we gathered outside the Dalai Lama's compound to await His Holiness's arrival and blessing. Surrounding us was a colorful assembly of Tibetans, Ladakhis, and Indians, all in native dress. Our Tibetan hosts had thoughtfully provided extra *khatas* — the long white ceremonial scarves Tibetans use on official occasions — and instructed us in the art of unfolding and offering them.

It is difficult to describe the feeling of reverence and

devotion with which these people regard their spiritual leader, just as it is difficult to convey anything of the special radiance of the Dalai Lama. At a quick glance the thirty-seven-year-old Lama resembled an ordinary monk wearing the simple red robes of his order. But one soon became aware of that indefinable aura which comes from years of preoccupation with spiritual matters and deep meditation. The Dalai Lama is said to be a reincarnation of Avalokitesvara, the Bodhisattva of Compassion. During a later private audience we found him to be not only compassionate and concerned about the plight of his own people but also interested in the social and political problems of the outside world. He was obviously trying to reconcile the complexities of a modern, technological world with the ideals of his Buddhist faith.

The first day of Losar is always devoted to prayers and meditation. The second day is the traditional time to visit relatives and friends and sip countless cups of salty butter tea or chang, the sake-like rice wine. On the third day we joined the crowds in an open-air theater in the forest for a whole-day performance of the Tibetan Music, Dance, and Drama Society. This group was organized with the support of the Dalai Lama in order to keep alive one of the most cherished artistic traditions of old Tibet—the singing minstrels and drama groups who enacted the ancient mystery plays and lives of Tibet's kings and sages.

The big prayer festival of Mönlam, during which many rare Tibetan Buddhist rituals were performed, started immediately after Losar. In the stillness of the early-morning hours we could hear the extraordinary chants of the Tantric monks. In Tibet the main centers of study in Gelugpa Tantric teachings were the colleges of Gyutö and Gyume in Lhasa. Some of their monks managed to escape to India, where they started a new Tantric college in Dalhousie near Dharamsala. We watched as they traced intricate mandalas on the ground on which to perform fire offerings, and we marveled at the exquisite butter sculptures they prepared for the temple.

The debates, another hallowed Tibetan tradition, took place below the temple in clear view of much of the village population. These religious and philosophical debates form part of the sophisticated training of Tibetan Buddhist monks. In a rather stylized ritual, candidates for the title of geshe, a sort of doctor of divinity, have to debate the fine points of Buddhist philosophy and metaphysics with their fellow lamas and monks. Although the lay people failed to catch the meaning of many of their witty replies, they thoroughly enjoyed the ritual.

At some point during this first lengthy stay in the Himalaya, we came to realize that while we had arrived strictly as tourists we were now getting emotionally involved in the fate of these beautiful, gentle people. Already we had been "adopted" by two foster children and felt a strong desire to learn more about Mahayana Buddhism. Thus started a long journey through most of the Buddhist regions of the Himalaya which was to take us to Kulu Valley and Ladakh, Nepal and Sikkim, Darjeeling, Kalimpong and Bhutan. We are still traveling.

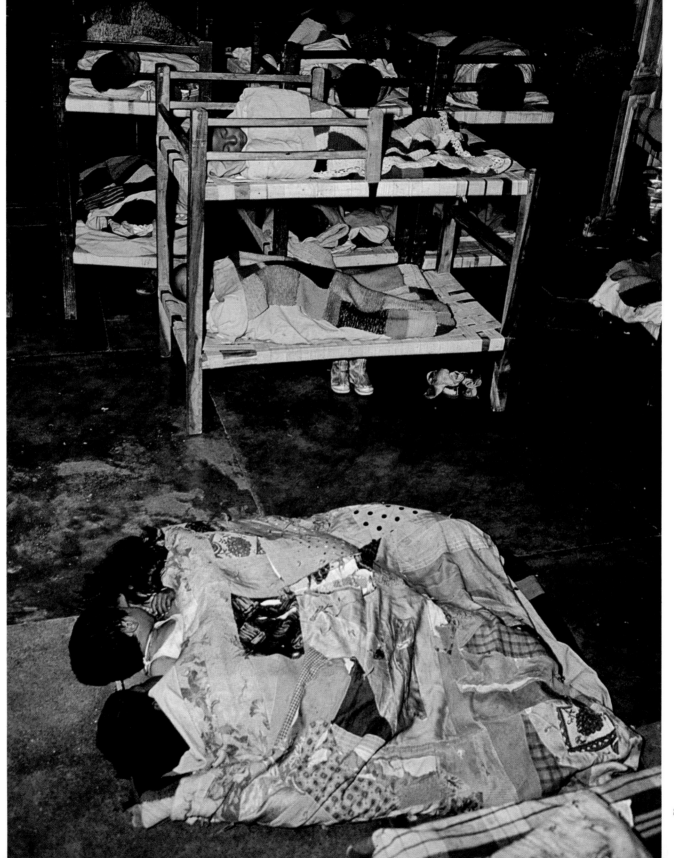

16

22

Mussoorie and Dharamsala

1 A happy group of Tibetan refugees in Dharamsala watching a performance of a traditional folk opera by the Tibetan Music, Dance, and Drama Society.

2,3,4 Elderly Tibetans who are being cared for in the old people's home in Mussoorie, and one of the new generation of Tibetans born in India.

5,6,7 During a performance of the Lhamo folk opera, a Lhasa Apso terrier was dressed up by children and found an immediate audience. Tibetans are always surrounded by their cuddly Apsos, whom they love and care for as they do their own children.

8,9,10 Young Tibetan children in the nursery of the Tibetan Children's Village in Upper Dharamsala and in the Tibetan Homes in Mussoorie during the annual picnic.

11,12,13 In Kulu Valley, north of Simla, in the state of Himachal Pradesh, entire families of Tibetan refugees work on road construction while their babies sleep peacefully along the road.

14 The roadworkers' camp, which changes location as the new road progresses. Kulu Valley, or the valley of the Beas River, is famous for its scenic beauty.

15 McLeod Ganj in Upper Dharamsala, one of the main refugee settlements and residence of His Holiness the Dalai Lama. In the central square refugees circumambulate a newly built *chörten*, or shrine, and keep the prayer wheels in the wall spinning continuously. The women wear the *chuba* and *pangden*, the

traditional long dress and colorful apron of the Central Tibetan province of Ü and the capital city of Lhasa.

16 Refugees returning from a festival to their humble huts in Dharamsala.

17 Tibetans in Dharamsala await the arrival of His Holiness the Dalai Lama on Losar (New Year's) morning.

18 The Dalai Lama steps out of his temple to bless the crowd.

19,20 It takes monk artists an entire day to trace the intricate mandala and fill it out with colored sand. These symbolic designs are used in different Tibetan Buddhist ceremonies. Here the mandala forms the base for a fire offering.

21 Tantric monks of Gyuto College perform a special rite in front of Namgyal Monastery in Dharamsala, during which they use the two sacred objects of Mahayana Buddhism, the *dorje* and the *dibu* — the thunderbolt and the bell — symbolizing wisdom and compassion.

22 A Tantric Lama pours ghee (clarified butter), various grains, seeds, and herbs into a fire during a fire *puja*, or purification rite. The fire was built on top of a mandala design.

23,24 Tantric monks in ceremonial robes chanting prayers in the temple of Namgyal Monastery in Dharamsala.

25,26 After the New Year's blessing by His Holiness the Dalai Lama, everybody is anxious to receive one of the ribbons given out by His Holiness. Many Tibetans will wear this ribbon tied around their necks for the rest of the year.

27 A monk artist with a just-completed butter sculpture, which will be placed in the temple as an offering.

28 Tibetans admire the beautiful and intricate butter sculptures in the Dalai Lama's temple during Mönlam, the big prayer festival during the first Tibetan month of the year (in early spring).

29,30 Three monks wearing ceremonial hats are being examined on their knowledge of Buddhist religion and philosophy by fellow monks. These public debates are conducted in a lively manner, with elaborate gestures and much hand-clapping.

31,32 A performance of the Lhamo folk opera by the Tibetan Music, Dance, and Drama Society of Dharamsala, which was founded by His Holiness the Dalai Lama in order to preserve this important aspect of Tibet's cultural heritage.

33 A prayer session in Namgyal Monastery in Dharamsala.

34 Lamas putting on their yellow robes after the prayer session.

35 A Tibetan explains the meaning of the Wheel of Life to his son in Manali, Kulu Valley.

Nepal

The first of the once-forbidden Himalayan kingdoms to open its doors to the outside world, Nepal has seen a veritable avalanche of tourists and young Western spiritual seekers roll through its peaceful valleys. But in 1976, when we visited here anew after a prolonged absence, we found that twenty years of exposure to often shockingly crude and commercial Western ways had not yet changed the basic nature of one of the most gentle, charming, and hospitable countries in Asia.

The landlocked nation of ten million people of varied ethnic backgrounds shares a long border with India and Tibet. For many centuries a Buddhist nation, Nepal, the birthland of Lord Buddha, is today a Hindu kingdom. Not only are both religions tolerated here, but they are practiced side by side and often fuse into a unique synthesis. Hindus have accepted Lord Buddha as the ninth incarnation of their god Vishnu, and Buddhist and Brahmanical gods coexist so harmoniously that the average Nepalese is often not even aware of the sectarian distinction.

Throughout its history Nepal has maintained close cultural bonds with India. Indian mythological traditions have found ready acceptance here, and the splendid aesthetic heritage of ancient Gupta art forms the basis of Nepalese art, which in turn strongly influenced the Buddhist art of Tibet and imperial China. Historic records tell us that the Mongolian emperor Kublai Khan, who ruled China during the thirteenth century A.D., asked the ruler of Western Tibet, the Lama-King of Sakya, to send him an artist to embellish the imperial chapel. The Tibetan abbot sent for Nepali artists, who were renowned for their skills. One of them, Aniko, not only spent many years at the imperial court in Peking but set artistic and iconometric norms which were subsequently followed by many Chinese painters and sculptors.

The cradle of Nepali culture is Katmandu Valley, situated on the middle level of this three-story country (the southern lowlands of the Terai consist mostly of swampy jungles, while the northern areas are formed by the high Himalayan ranges). The inhabitants of the valley, the Newaris, have long been famous for their artistic gifts. The entire valley, with its countless temples, shrines, palaces, and ordinary dwellings, is one of the largest outdoor museums in the world. Months would be needed to appreciate fully the architectural and artistic treasures of Katmandu and the nearby cities of Patan and Bhaktapur, of ancient temples like Swayambhunath and Pashupatinath, Changu Narayan and Bodhnath.

Bodhnath, a short ride from Katmandu, centers around the white dome of a giant stupa, a Buddhist shrine, whose all-seeing eyes survey the valley in every direction. A tall spire rises from its center in thirteen diminishing squares and is crowned by the symbols of Mahayana Buddhism. Built by a Buddhist king of the Licchavi Dynasty about 500 A.D., Bodhnath has long been one of the holy places visited by Tibetan pilgrims on the way to Lumbini and Bodhgaya. Since 1959 hundreds of Tibetan refugees have settled around the stupa, where they have created a picturesque Tibetan enclave. The four Tibetan Buddhist orders of Nyingmapa, Sakyapa, Kagyupa, and Gelugpa have all established new monasteries nearby, thus providing an infusion of new life into the older Buddhist traditions of the valley. It is here that most young Western people look for spiritual teachings.

There is another entirely different world in the high Himalaya where the legendary Sherpas still live much the way Tibetans used to live on their windswept plateau. A single-engine plane took us from Katmandu over the foothills to the tiny airfield at Lukla, 9500 feet high, which Sir Edward Hillary and his Sherpa friends quite literally stamped out of the ground. From there it is a two-day trek through pine forests and rhododendron thickets to Namche Bazaar, the heart of Solokhumbo, or "Sherpaland."

Made famous as the tough mountaineering guides and porters of many Himalayan expeditions, the Sherpas are closely related to the Tibetans, speak a Tibetan dialect, and are devout followers of Tibetan Buddhism. They supposedly migrated here several centuries ago from Kham in Eastern Tibet and have tried to eke out a living under severe climatic conditions. Like Khampa nomads, these mountain people have been formed by their harsh environment and their Buddhist faith. Strong and independent, patient and even-tempered, with rugged, handsome features, they are highly respected by all foreign mountaineers.

We were lucky to secure as a guide for a three-week high-altitude trek one of the outstanding Sherpa guides in Namche, Ila Tsering, who had climbed Mount Everest with Dyhrenfurth in 1963. His thirteen-year-old son, Tsering Wangdi, stopped us in the bazaar by asking Ernst Haas in fluent English, "Are you from England?" "No, I am from Austria." "Oh, that's near Hungary, isn't it?" We were astounded, since most people in Asia somehow associate Austria with kangaroos. "Where did you learn English?" "In my school in Khumjung village." (This model school was started by Sir Edmund and his friends.) "And who told you about Austria?" "My father did, he was in Europe. He also visited the king of America!"

Ila Tsering, who had met "King" Kennedy, following the Dyhrenfurth expedition, came to inspect our trekking gear and went shopping with us in the bazaar for provisioning that would augment the barley flour and potato diet of the villagers. There is plenty of variety in the Namche "delicatessen." Every international expedition unloads excess baggage after the climb, and smoked oysters and other seafood delicacies from Japan and canned meat and vegetables from Europe sit next to peanut butter and other snacks from America. We stocked our food chest and set off in the direction of Thame along the ancient trade route to Tibet. Normal access to Tibet is blocked, but Sherpa traders are occasionally allowed into Southern Tibet strictly for commerce.

Along the Bhote River the trail goes up and down and around numerous *chörtens,* or Buddhist stupas. The direction around them is always clockwise, and the prayer mills in the wall must also be turned clockwise. Along the road pass caravans of burdened yaks, those shaggy Himalayan beasts that provide the mountain people with their meat and milk, hides, fuel, companionship, and transport. The owners talk to their yaks or dris (the female of the species), caress them, admonish them as we would our dogs. Tsering Wangdi burst out laughing when asked whether he takes yak butter in his tea. There is nothing funny about butter tea, but *yak* butter? Really! How could a male yak produce butter? Anyway, there was plenty of *pö cha* — Tibetan tea with butter and salt — a most welcome and nourishing drink after a day in the mountains. It tastes rather like bouillon.

Two days in Thame gave us the long-awaited chance to see how the people live at high altitude in their simple stone houses built around ancient Buddhist shrines. Most houses are stables and granaries as well as dwellings. The animals occupy the ground floor, and the kitchen and living area are on the second floor. Houses of the well-to-do might have a small prayer room and bedrooms above. Family life centers around the hearth, where a hot pot of tea seems always to be ready. And during much of the year, when an icy wind howls outside, it is good to fall asleep under yak-hair covers near the fire. The people of these valleys are cheerful and hospitable, share their supper of fried potatoes or barley soup with visitors, and love to tell stories of the *yeti,* the mysterious abominable snowman whom nobody has ever caught but whom many villagers swear they have seen.

Little Tsering Wangdi was dying to show us proof that this elusive creature really exists, so on another trek eastbound toward the base camp of Mount Everest we stopped at Pangboche Monastery, below the towering peak of Amadablam, the sacred mountain of the Sherpas. A kindly old Lama opened the door of the extravagantly decorated upper chambers of the gompa, allowing us a glimpse of a red hairy animal scalp and a large hand. Tsering Wangdi giggled nervously. His father told us the story of two girls from Khumjung who had been attacked by such a creature during a stormy night on one of the high meadows. All their yaks had been killed by the *yeti* while the terrified girls managed to run off. American scientists who have tested the scalp say it is that of a rare Tibetan blue bear, but the legends will not die.

Surely one of the most beautiful settings in Sherpaland, if not in the whole world, is that of Thangboche, the lovely Buddhist monastery high above the thunderous torrent of the Imja River. Behind it rise the white giants of the Himalaya whose grandeur and purity help explain the intense religious feelings of the people living below them. Everest is not nearly the most spectacular of these mountains, nor does it seem noticeably higher than neighboring Lhotse or Nhuptse. Amadablam, rising dramatically out of the valley like a Himalayan Matterhorn, is much more striking. But Everest, with its long plume of snow streaming from the summit like a prayer flag, exerts its own fascination. To Tibetans it is known as Jomolangmo, the sacred abode of the goddess Tseringma.

Snow falling during the evening hours soon blanketed the tents on the yak meadow below Thangboche. We decided to pay a visit to the monastery. There the venerable head Lama led the assembly of monks in the chanting of evening prayers. As in most Himalayan countries, the monks are supported by the population. When a family is too poor to feed another mouth, the mother will gladly send her son to the monastery, knowing that his physical and spiritual needs will be well taken care of.

Amazing treasures can be found in these dim chapels: ancient bronzes, *thankas* (scroll paintings), and rare Buddhist manuscripts. Thangboche is not old—the original building was leveled during an earthquake—but its walls are adorned with the most exquisite frescoes and miniature paintings.

When we came out into the cold night, the snow had stopped and a brilliant moon was rising over the distant peaks and glaciers. Ila Tsering was singing a melancholy song in his tent; a soft tinkling came from tiny pearls attached to the pinnacle of the nearby *chörten;* prayer flags gently sent the everlasting message of the Buddha into the four directions: *OM MANI PADME HUM.*

Bhutan

Of all the Himalayan countries only Bhutan has been able to retain completely its native identity and to withstand the leveling influence of the industrial societies right up to the 1970s.

Barely a generation ago one still spoke of the "three forbidden kingdoms" of Nepal, Sikkim, and Bhutan. The more remote and "forbidden" a country was said to be, the more determined outsiders were to crash its doors. Today we deplore the "Westernization" of Nepal and Sikkim but at the same time chide Bhutan for not opening its doors wide to a similar onslaught of foreign tourists and commerce.

Bhutan has practiced the art of aloofness for centuries. This picturesque kingdom the size of Switzerland is completely surrounded by Tibetan China and India and has often had to fight off invaders from both sides. Much like the Swiss, the Bhutanese have stubbornly defended their mountainous homeland and are asking only to be left alone so that they may come to their own — gradual — accommodation with the twentieth century.

When the young king of Bhutan, His Majesty Jigme Singye Wangchuk, was crowned in June 1974, the Himalayan country for the first time opened its doors to some three hundred selected foreign guests and the international press. Those of us lucky enough to have been invited witnessed a rare display of Oriental pageantry. From the moment we crossed the border until the moment eight days later when we returned to India, we had the feeling of being transported back in time to an enchanting fairy-tale country where all is beauty and serenity.

From the border town of Phuntsoling we were escorted along a recently built hardtop road through dense pine forests, across misty mountain passes and bubbly streams to the capital city of Thimphu, 179 miles away. On the way we stopped in beautiful Paro Valley to visit an ancient dzong, one of the combination fortresses and monasteries which command most of Bhutan's valleys from their strategic hilltop locations. Stern and medieval-looking on the outside, these retreats usually house several chapels exquisitely decorated with scenes of Buddhist mythology.

A little farther up the valley we had a glimpse of Taktshang Monastery, the "Tiger's Lair." Bhutanese believe that Padmasambhava, the Indian mystic who brought Buddhism to Bhutan and Tibet during the eighth century A.D., landed here on a flying tiger. One needs wings indeed to reach this tiny shrine perched high on a sheer cliff!

Buddhism permeates everything in Bhutan, as it does in neighboring Tibet. The two peoples are closely related by blood ties and a common culture and language. Most Bhutanese belong to the Drukpa Kagyupa sect of Tibetan Buddhism, which also gave the country its name: Druk Yul. The Bhutanese call themselves Drukpas, the "Dragon People."

Before entering Thimphu, we passed the oldest of all the dzongs, Simtokha Dzong, and its famous lama school. The capital itself is dominated by the even more formidable Tashichodzong, residence of the chief Lama, His Holiness Je Khenpo, and seat of the royal government.

Throughout the country, houses are built in traditional Bhutanese style. Elaborately carved and painted upper structures are topped by an open double roof used for drying crops. Thick walls give shelter from the fierce cold winds that blow down these valleys from the high Tibetan plateau during the winter months.

But in June, when Bhutan celebrated the coronation of its young king, a mild summer breeze carried the scent of pines and roses across Thimphu Valley. The small town was an explosion of colors as myriads of flowers competed with multicolored Buddhist symbols and prayer flags.

When the much-beloved late King Jigme Dorji Wangchuk met with an untimely death in 1972, his only son was sixteen years old. But the crown prince had for years been carefully groomed by his father and had received additional training abroad. Once the date for the coronation had been set by a court astrologer, the whole country went to work preparing for this important event. Artists and craftsmen came from all over the kingdom to help erect new buildings and embellish others. New uniforms of the unique hand-woven Bhutanese cloth were tailored for all officials. Delicacies which could not be prepared locally were ordered from India. And every schoolboy with a knowledge of English was sent to the capital to help welcome and serve the guests. Even the members of the royal family and the aristocracy were pressed into service to act as hostesses and liaison officers. As the day of the important event approached, the Lamas moved into the mountains surrounding Thimphu to perform religious rites that would ensure good weather during the coronation. (They were obviously successful! The monsoon rains held off until the day after the last ceremony.)

Once begun, the festivities proceeded with great style. From the morning of the actual coronation inside the venerable Tashichodzong, to the last state dinner given under a brilliant night sky, every hour was filled with carefully orchestrated processions, ceremonials, dances, games, and receptions, each more glittering than the last. Among the guests were members of the diplomatic corps from Delhi and dignitaries from four continents, as well as high lamas and ordinary Bhutanese who had come down from their mountain villages by the thousands. It was a charmingly intimate yet formal event which brought out the best in the hospitable Bhutanese. They quite obviously adored their young, good-looking king, who goes to great lengths to stay in close touch with the people, as his father did before him. Once the more formal ceremonies were finished, the king joined other young Bhutanese and foreign diplomats in an archery contest. This immensely popular national sport was also a favorite of King Jigme Dorji Wangchuk, who reportedly, during a 1962 border skirmish, held off the Chinese for one week in the high mountain passes accompanied by men armed only with bows and arrows. After that, India had to help him with modern arms, but a dangerous crisis was averted.

The late king was greatly respected abroad, but his young son had yet to prove himself. His first test came as he faced a dozen senior reporters from the world's leading news agencies after his coronation. Refusing to be intimidated, he answered their questions openly and with great aplomb. He assured them that he would continue the policies of his late father who, as a liberal and humanitarian, abolished serfdom and worked toward democratization of the royalty, emancipation of women, land reforms, participation in international organizations (Bhutan is a member of the United Nations), and economic self-reliance. May he be allowed to put his idealism to work. Bhutan needs a strong and mature leader if it is to hold its own and preserve its ethnic identity.

63   64

68

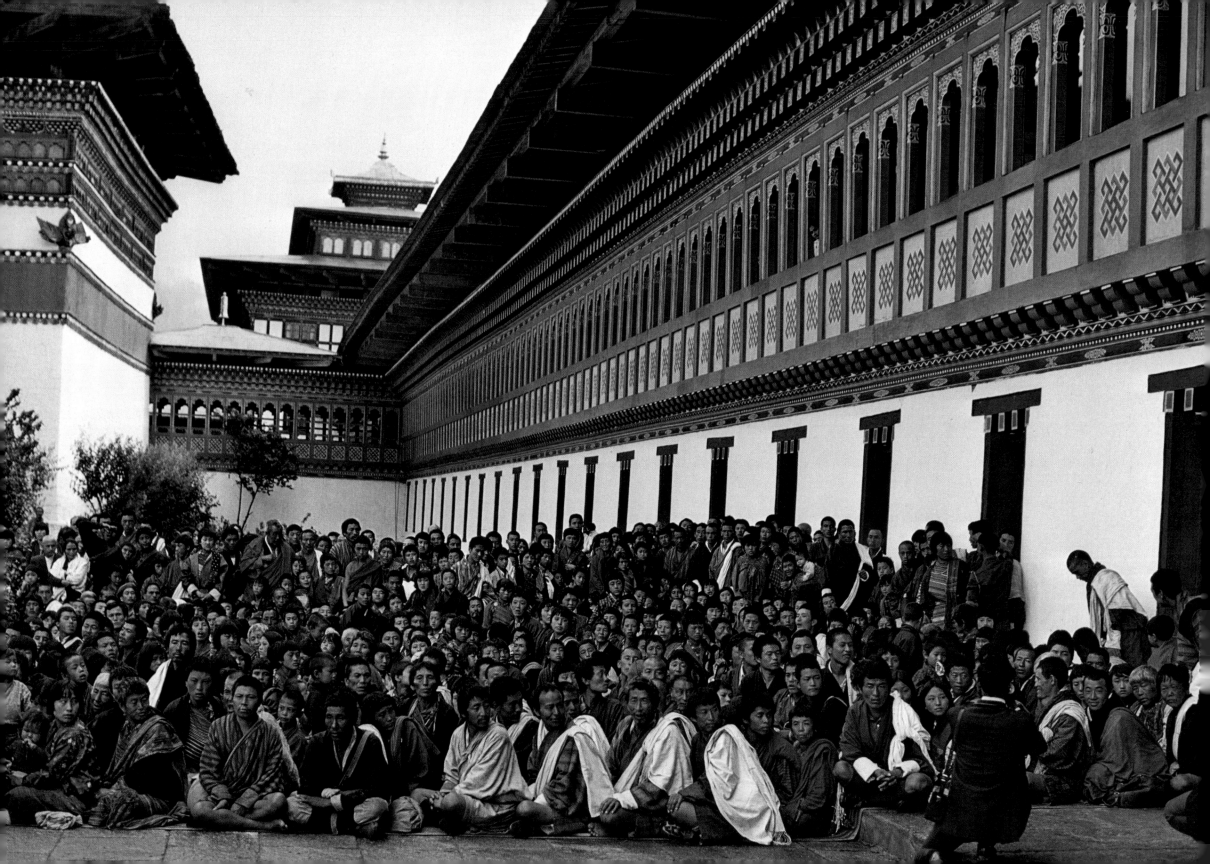

81

Bhutan

60 Tashichodzong in Thimphu, seat of the Royal Government of Bhutan, where the coronation of King Jigme Singye Wangchuk took place.

61,62 The coronation began with a colorful procession through the capital city of Thimphu to Tashichodzong Castle, where thousands of spectators awaited the arrival of the young king and foreign guests.

63 The Queen Mother of Bhutan, Her Royal Highness Ashi Kesang, the princesses, and other members of the royal family arrive for the coronation.

64 The then president of India, Mr. Giri, and his wife being welcomed to Tashichodzong.

65,66 The great courtyard of Tashichodzong Castle, where dancers performed ceremonial dances, while monks on the roof heralded the arrival of His Majesty the King.

67,68 Coronation guests arrive at Tashichodzong bearing their gifts for the young king.

69 Local guests awaiting the arrival of the young king inside the castle.

70 His Majesty King Jigme Singye Wangchuk receives well-wishers after the coronation, who place *khatas,* long white silk scarves, in front of him as a sign of respect. The many valuable coronation presents are displayed on a table facing him.

71 A huge appliquéd *thanka* in Tashichodzong depicting the Indian Guru Padmasambhava, who brought Buddhism to Bhutan in the eighth century A.D.

72 Dancers perform for the guests in the courtyard of Tashichodzong. At the spectacular climax they leap high into the air in unison.

73 Bhutanese folk dancers from different provinces arrive at Tashichodzong.

74 Dancers arrange their costumes before a performance of folk dances.

75 Small monks try on masks in preparation for a mystery play to be performed for the royal guests.

76 One of the magnificent brocade costumes worn by the dancers. The little Bhutanese boy wears the traditional *khirra,* the national costume, made of colorful hand-loomed wool.

77 Monks perform the traditional black-hat dance in the grounds of Changli-mithang Stadium in Thimphu, capital of Bhutan.

78 An archery contest by the local people in Thimphu.

79 His Majesty King Jigme Singye Wangchuk in an archery contest with His Highness Palden Thondup Namgyal, the Chogyal of Sikkim.

80 His Majesty King Jigme Singye Wangchuk with his sister, Her Royal Highness Ashi Dechen Wangmo.

81 The beautiful Queen Mother, Her Royal Highness Ashi Kesang.

82 A monk blowing on a thigh bone, a symbol of the impermanence of all things.

Ladakh

"Lesser Tibet"

When the Government of India decided in 1974 to open the remote district of Ladakh to visitors, the news was enthusiastically received around the world. For this cul-de-sac in the northernmost corner of India represents one of the few remaining strongholds of Tibetan culture.

Once part of Western Tibet, this wild and beautiful land has seen invasions by Dards, Moguls, and Sikhs. In 1947 it officially became part of Kashmir and thus a part of the Indian Union. The different cultures have all left a distinct imprint on Ladakh. Today the western part is racially akin to Kashmir and Turkistan and bows its head to Mecca, while people of the eastern part have predominantly Mongolian features and follow Tibetan Buddhist traditions.

Of the two motorable roads leading to Ladakh the more spectacular one, the "highest road in the world," which connects Kulu Valley and Lahul/Spiti with the Upper Indus Valley via 17,500-foot-high passes, is not open to tourists. The other road from Srinagar in the Vale of Kashmir winds its way for 245 miles up the Sind Valley, across snowed-in Zojila and two more high-altitude passes through some of the most forbidding country on earth. It is not an easy trip, but the experienced Himalayan traveler will find it a thrilling two-day journey.

At Zoji Pass, where the last traces of Kashmir's lush vegetation recede, one enters a moonscape of windswept plateaus and mountain peaks soaring as high as four miles. For the most part inhospitable and craggy, the terrain is arid beyond belief. Burning heat by day is followed by piercing cold at night. The annual rainfall rarely exceeds three to four inches. Not surprisingly, there are few signs of human life; marmots, mountain goats, and eagles are more at home in this desolate world.

Beyond Kargil, Ladakh's second-largest town with barely three thousand souls, one enters the Buddhist world. The new hardtop road closely follows the ancient trade route to Central Asia along which Buddhist sages from India carried the teachings of Sakyamuni Buddha to Western Tibet. The renowned Buddhist saint Naropa is said to have stopped at Lamayuru, the ancient, mysterious lamasery on the slopes of Fatu Pass. The great translator Lochen Rinchen Zangpo was instrumental in the construction of numerous eleventh-century shrines on both sides of the Upper Indus, notably the artistic masterpiece of Alchi just west of Leh.

Leh, Ladakh's capital city, lies on a high plateau of granite dust between the Indus and the Ladakh range of mountains. A compact town of about 8500 people, it is dominated by the "castle," an impressive structure looking almost like a smaller version of the Potala in Lhasa. The whole town has a Tibetan air about it, with its flat-roofed, whitewashed houses that cling to each other and lean fortress-like into the wind. Until the Chinese take-over of Tibet in the 1950s, the focal point of this trans-Himalayan bazaar was Lhasa rather than the Westernized Indian centers. Today the trade routes are cut, reducing Leh to a sleepy outpost on the edge of the free world.

When our jeep roared up Leh's main street, we were immediately engulfed by a shouting mass of children, Ladakhi and Kashmiri traders, Tibetan refugees, and Indian army officers. They had taken our vehicle for an advance column of the procession that was slowly winding its way up the serpentine bends behind us. We had barely time to look around this utterly exotic bazaar before we were whisked off to a vantage point to watch the arrival of the new Rinpoche, the thirteen-year-old boy who was to become head Lama of the famous Hemis Gompa.

Apparently the abbot of this nearby monastery of the Drukpa Kagyupa order of Tibetan Buddhism had made a pilgrimage to Tibet many years ago and had never been heard from again. His lamasery had thus been without a head Lama ever since. But recently a *tulku* had been discovered—a reincarnation in the person of a small Tibetan monk in one of the monasteries in Darjeeling. The thirteen-year-old boy showed all the proper signs and attributes predicted by the oracle and was now being led in procession up the Indus Valley to his new abode. The villagers were ecstatic as his jeep, decorated with yellow and red garlands, became visible on the outskirts of Leh. Decked out in their finest clothes and jewelry, the villagers lined the streets, bearing symbolic offerings of barley flower and tea. A serious, handsome young face looked at us over the windshield of an open jeep, seemingly unperturbed by the commotion. Tibetans believe that *tulkus* are no ordinary children. We came to believe it while observing the mature demeanor of the young Drukpa Rinpoche during the following Hemis Festival.

Hemis Monastery, built during the seventeenth century A.D., miraculously escaped the fate of many older Buddhist shrines in Ladakh that were destroyed by Muslim invaders. Hidden high up a side valley of the Indus, it was well protected by forests and rocks and managed to preserve its priceless treasures of Buddhist art and manuscripts.

Crowds of Ladakhi and Tibetan pilgrims led the way to Hemis across the dark-blue Indus and up a rockstrewn, windswept slope. For about a mile the route followed one of the longest "*mani* walls" in existence—one of those ridges typical of the Buddhist Himalaya that bear testimony to the faith of a continuous flow of pious pilgrims who have placed thousands of stone slabs bearing the sacred syllables one on top of the other. Once inside the narrow gully of a mountain stream, we could hear the bellowing of conch shells announcing the beginning of the Hemis Tsichu, or annual festival. We hurried through

an ancient gate, seeking seats inside the main courtyard of the monastery just as the mystery play was about to start.

Held on the tenth day of the fifth Buddhist month—usually in May or June—the Hemis Tsichu honors the birthday of Padmasambhava, the founder of the ancient mystic order of the Nyingmapa, who combined the teachings of Buddha with elements of the earlier shamanistic Bön cult native to these Himalayan regions.

Each year the monks reenact scenes from Tibetan Buddhist mythology in the form of a slow-motion, ritual "lama dance" that goes on for two days. The elaborate costumes and masks, even the steps and hand gestures, are in strict accordance with Lamaist traditions going back hundreds of years. So ancient and valuable are the brocade costumes that they are stored between layers of silk gauze in sandalwood chests and taken out only once a year.

Ladakhis and Tibetans know every step and gesture of the play, as we know the scenes from the Nativity. For them it is as much a religious rite as a spectacle, and they sit enraptured for hours on end under a scorching sun. Little children scream with fear when some of the fiercer-looking creatures of the *bardo,* the mysterious no-man's-land between death and rebirth, make their appearance. And they laugh out loud at the small monks who provide comic interludes by acting out the humorous aspects of monastic life. The young Rinpoche seated on brocade cushions below a huge scroll painting of Padmasambhava obviously enjoyed this first contact with his new monastic community.

High among the surrounding mountains is ancient Gotsang Gompa, a hermit's retreat perched at an altitude of 13,000 feet. Tibetan Buddhism in general and the red-hat sect in particular emphasize the merits of prolonged periods of solitary meditation, a practice which can be maintained only in quiet, sparsely populated areas and in a monastic tradition that allows for other monks to take care of the meditator's basic needs. Initiates are locked into bare cells, usually for several years, and are given food and drink through a small opening by one of their fellow monks. At that time, a number of adepts were in deep meditation and would stay for three years, three months, and three days behind the walls of the exquisite Tibetan-style shrine.

Watching the sun rise over tier after tier of great, bare, lonely mountaintops, one feels some of the bliss which the combination of quietude, altitude, and unspoiled nature can bring about. What a blessed country, where old traditions are still respected, where every sentient being is still sacred, where people are still able to listen to the voice of nature!

With the exception of the Hemis Tsichu, almost all important festivals in Ladakh take place during the long winter months when the barley fields are frozen and the yak herders and their beasts are in the valley. The hardy Ladakhis then brave the bitter cold, bundled up in shaggy furs and warm, hand-stitched felt boots, to attend the many popular celebrations.

Beginning around December with the Ladakhi New Year, the local population follows an alternately jolly and solemn round of secular and monastic holidays. During Leh Dosmoche the bazaar closes down for three days while young and old watch a colorful procession, which is followed by the burning of the *storma* — effigies in various sizes representing men and demons. The Buddhist or Tibetan New Year in early spring is celebrated with much chang by the Tibetan community in Leh, while Khampa horsemen and nomads from the high plateau of Changtang perform their native dances and display their skills in horsemanship along the Indus River. With the Tibetan border only scant miles away, many an elderly refugee is seen brushing away tears of nostalgia during the festival.

All the monasteries in the hills around Leh hold

some sort of annual celebration. Most extraordinary of all is the Matho festival. According to Tibetan legends, a Lama of the Sakya order from Kham in Eastern Tibet moved to this area many, many generations ago to establish a new monastery. A good spirit by the name of Khawa Karpro (White Snow) followed him all the way to take up residence in the new gompa. Once a year two oracles go into deep meditation and eventually into a trance in White Snow's chamber. The spirit of Khawa Karpro and that of Khor, his attendant, then enter their bodies, sending them out to perform dramatic feats and to make prophecies concerning the villagers. This extraordinary spectacle is followed with awe by thousands of Ladakhis and Tibetans. Crowded into the courtyards, onto the roofs, and onto every available ledge of the monastery, they shriek with fear and hide their heads when the two ferocious-looking, blindfolded oracles suddenly jump barefoot from one dizzying cornice to another or right into their midst. Even we were overcome with apprehension, if not to say horror, at the sight of the oracles' repeated attempts to cut their tongues with swords, sending trickles of blood down their necks. They panted like wild animals, roared like dragons, and looked every bit as fierce as the wrathful deities depicted inside the temple. Every now and then we had to look up at the majestic, snow-covered peaks around us or the distant, lonely contrail of a jet plane to remind ourselves that we were still in the twentieth century.

When only a few days later a heavy military transport plane slowly lifted us off the banks of the Indus and circled right above the flat roofs of Spituk Gompa we knew that we had witnessed some of the magic of ancient Tibet, some of the mysterious mixture of pre-Buddhist "Bön Chö," with its superstitions and bloody rites and the pure teachings of Lord Buddha as it still survives in these remote mountain areas. Climbing and circling steadily to twenty-thousand feet, we looked north over the barren high plateau of Tibet and south over the matchless white expanse of the highest mountains and glaciers of our planet. Altitude and solitude seem to lead to similar reflections on the fleeting nature of all things and the futility of our material existence. With our faces pressed against the window panes we looked down on the lands where these reflections found such powerful and universally appealing exponents in the persons of great sages such as Buddha.

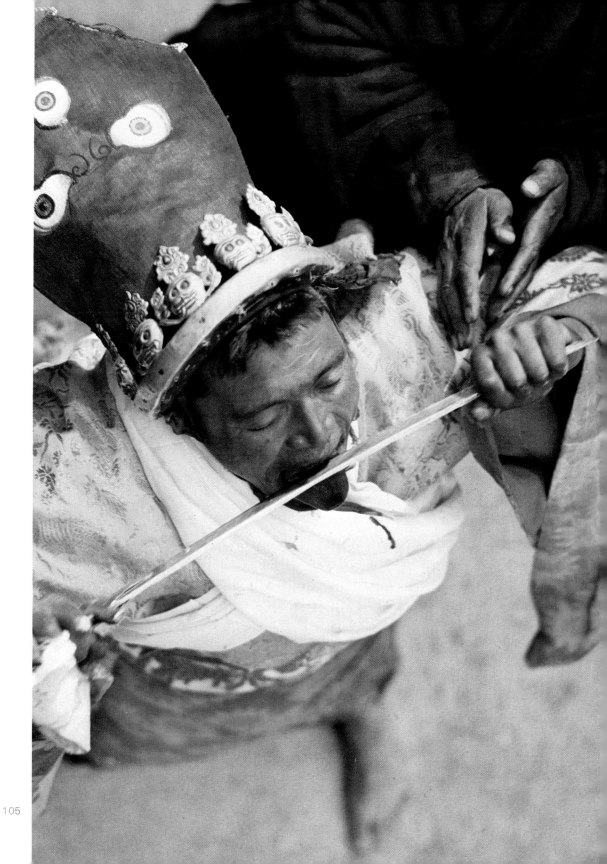

Ladakh

83 The barren landscape of Central Ladakh along the Srinagar-Leh road, with Buddhist *chörtens* in the foreground.

84 The eleventh-century lamasery of Lama Yuru below Fatu pass. The strange geological formation in the background testifies to the existence of a former lake which broke through its natural rocky dam and emptied into the Indus Valley.

85 A Ladakhi peasant heading home from the barren plateau with her small herd of dzos.

86 Old wall paintings in Hemis Monastery, depicting the life of a Buddhist sage.

87 Small monks paint the windows of Lama Yuru monastery with the traditional black border in preparation for the annual festival.

88 The altar with an image of Vairocana in Alchi Gompa.

89 One of the magnificent murals in Alchi, depicting the eleven-headed Avalokitesvara.

90,91,92 A Ladakhi man wearing the traditional stovepipe hat; a Tibetan woman and her child from the Chang Tang area; a wealthy Ladakhi woman wearing her heirloom turquoise jewelry in the form of a headdress called *peyrac*.

93 Ladakhis gather on the rocky slopes above Leh to watch the lama dances in a monastery courtyard. Above, on Namgyal Peak, is the seventeenth-century palace fort of King Sengay Namgyal.

94 During the annual Leh Dosmoche masked monks perform an ancient ritual in which a symbolic effigy of evil forces is being destroyed.

95,96 Following the lama dances, the people of Leh walk back to town from the hilltop castle.

97,98 Below Leh Castle a joyous crowd surrounds masked dancers to watch the ritual burning of the *storma*. After the fire Ladakhi men gather the leftovers, which are said to ensure good luck for the coming year.

99,100 The new abbot of Hemis, thirteen-year old Drukpa Rinpoche, is being welcomed to his new monastery. The huge telescopic trumpets being blown by monks give out a deep, sonorous sound much like a Swiss alphorn.

101,102 Masked lama dancers during the annual Hemis Tsichu, when scenes from the life of Guru Padmasambhava are enacted.

103,104,105 During the annual festival at Stok Monastery, a figure symbolizing wisdom and compassion destroys a small effigy representing the human ego. The Stok oracle threatens to cut off his tongue.

106,107 Villagers watch in awe as the Stok oracles jump from roof to roof.

108,109 The two oracles at Stok shout out their prophecies while in a trance.

110,111 A group of elderly Ladakhis watch the two monk oracles at Matho Gompa, an ancient monastery of the Sakya order. One of the oracles is threatening to cut off his hand and is being begged by frightened villagers not to do so.

112,113 The two Matho oracles, blindfolded, are said to see through the eyes of the spirits painted on their bodies while they run around the monastery and the valley.

114 The view from the top of Spituk Monastery across the Upper Indus Valley toward Chang Tang and Tibet.

115 The long wall of *mani* stones leading up to Hemis Monastery.

116 View over Leh bazaar and the Zanskar ranges through a line of prayer flags fluttering outside the hilltop castle.

The Kalachakra Initiation

They came by train and bus, in open trucks or in crowded jeeps, on horseback or on foot: thousands and tens of thousands of pilgrims from all parts of the Himalaya, crowded into the village of Bodhgaya in India's state of Bihar. At the beginning of our Himalayan travels, four years earlier, they would have looked to us like one mass of Mongolian faces. Having wandered around their lands and lived among them, we could now easily tell the aristocratic Sikkimese from the broad-faced Bhutanese, the Khampa Tibetan with his long braids from the Ladakhi, the bewigged Mönpa tribesman from the light-skinned Nepalese.

For more than a year the talk in all Buddhist communities along the Himalayan range had centered around the *Wang,* the Dhukor Wangchen, also known by its Sanskrit name of Kalachakra, or the sermon on the Wheel of Time. Now it was about to start, with the Dalai Lama himself conducting the initiation right here in the holiest place of Buddhism. What exactly was this Kalachakra Initiation? Why was it so important to every Tibetan Buddhist? And why was it so rarely performed?

The teachings of the Kalachakra Tantra are said to have been given by Lord Buddha himself to a group of initiates in South India some 2500 years ago. For centuries the precepts were transmitted orally from teacher to carefully chosen disciple and were considered among the most esoteric and important of all Buddhist teachings. During the eleventh century A.D., at a time when Buddhism was beginning to decline in India proper, the Kalachakra Tantra was brought to Tibet by the renowned Indian sage and guru Atisa. Since then the doctrine has been passed on in an unbroken lineage right down to the present and fourteenth Dalai Lama.

In the old days, in Tibet, no lay people could ever

have hoped to receive these teachings. They were propagated solely among Lamas in the course of their initiation into the Vajrayana or Tantric school of Tibetan Buddhism. About the turn of the century a tradition was established whereby each Dalai Lama would conduct the initiation publicly a few times during his lifetime. Due to the doctrine's esoteric nature, most lay people would still not be able to understand the many different levels of meaning; however, merely to be present, to have the right attitude and motivation during the ceremony, was considered an important step on the path toward enlightenment.

Followers of Tantra believe that great teachings should not be preached until the five proper factors coincide: the proper time, the teacher, the place, the teaching, and the proper listener. In this case the time was considered most opportune, since, according to the Tibetan interpretation of the cosmic cycle, ours is the age of Kaliyoga, or degeneration, when teachings like these are of the utmost importance. Thus the Dalai Lama was imparting these teachings for the fifth time in his fairly young life and would do so once more within a few years.

As for the place, there could not be a more auspicious setting than that of Bodhgaya, the "place of the Buddha." It was here, under the legendary pipal or fig tree, that Lord Buddha attained enlightenment and release from the sorrowful round of existence after much searching and suffering. In nearby Sarnath he preached his first sermon. And his message eventually spread all across Asia from the great Buddhist university of Nalanda, which was once located not far from here.

For much of the year Bodhgaya is a small, sleepy village built around the old Mahabodhi Temple complex. During important Buddhist holidays the village often swells to double its size as pilgrims from all over the world come to visit the holy shrines. But nobody had ever seen a gathering here like the one we were about to witness. For two weeks the stream of arriving pilgrims increased until every available space in the village itself and a radius of about a mile around it was taken up. Tented camps sprang up along the dried-out riverbed. The State Government of Bihar had its hands full controlling traffic, sanitary conditions, and the supply of food and drinking water. Quite a few people died from exhaustion and exposure before the ceremony even started.

Our Lama friends helped us find accommodations in one of the tents. We were to share this makeshift inn with fifteen other pilgrims from various Himalayan countries. Much to our surprise, we counted at least forty bodies one night when the nocturnal prayer chants of our roommates awoke us. There were sleeping bags all over the floor, amid luggage, pots, and pans, but by the first light of dawn they had disappeared.

His Holiness the Dalai Lama arrived from his residence-in-exile in the mountains of Himachal Pradesh, accompanied by a retinue of high Lamas. He brought a large *thanka*—an exquisite Tibetan scroll painting. Depicting the Kalachakra deity, the *thanka* had been painted especially for the occasion by Tibetan artists. It was hung behind the Dalai Lama's seat, and while he retired to devote some time to meditation and prayer, several monk artists traced a mandala next to it out of colored sand. This delicate and beautiful cosmic diagram, a sort of ground plan of the spiritual world, would serve as an aid in meditation and visualization, together with the *thanka*. Much like symbolic American-Indian sand paintings, it had to be destroyed at the end of the ceremony.

During the first three days of the *Wang* the Dalai Lama prepared his audience for the actual initiation. From an elevated, canopied throne he addressed the *sanga*, or assembly of monks, and a veritable ocean of devout pilgrims stretching in all directions. Unable to follow his words, we could only watch and marvel at the congregation's patience and serenity during hours and hours of sermons, which ended at sunset with rhythmic prayer chants.

The fourth day was set aside as a day of rest, giving everybody an opportunity to visit the holy places and see their friends. We witnessed touching scenes as Tibetans suddenly spotted long-lost relatives. Brothers found each other again for the first time since leaving Tibet, grandparents saw their grandchildren for the first time, and many a pretty Bhutanese or Nepalese girl caught the eye of a would-be suitor. No big gathering in Asia is complete without a bazaar, and one soon grew around a few tables in an open field. Everything from religious mementos to antique Tibetan objects was offered for sale— often out of a dire need to pay for the return trip. Enterprising local beggars also managed to profit from the mellow spirit of the occasion.

During the moonlit nights a steady stream of pilgrims wandered around the central Mahabodhi Temple, prayer wheels spinning. As they did so, they placed candles on every wall and ledge; together with thousands of butter lamps, the candles gave the temple a most beautiful halo. At the same time, the shuffling of feet, the murmuring of the sacred mantra, *Om Mani Padme Hum,* and the ringing of temple bells blended into a pious litany.

Then the actual Kalachakra Initiation began. The Dalai Lama delivered a three-day discourse on Tantric Buddhism to a hushed and utterly attentive audience. For eight hours each day he spoke almost without interruption. And for eight hours his followers sat cross-legged, old and young, oblivious to heat and dust. Except during moments of meditation they never took their eyes off their spiritual leader. While rosaries and prayer wheels were turned with one hand, babies were gently rocked or tea bottles quietly passed on with the other. And there was silence, enough silence for the gentle, soothing voice to be heard clear across the field as His Holiness led his congregation through ritual after ritual and symbolically invested a high Lama with all the attributes of a Tantric priest. At one point, the initiates were told to place a red band across their eyes and the seed of the champaka flower on their foreheads, symbolizing the opening of the third or wisdom eye. Later, monks attired in elaborate brocade robes, gilded masks, and ornaments of carved animal bone performed a slow, ritual lama dance around the mandala to the accompaniment of a deep, monotonous chant. This sacred dance is said to represent a higher meditation and to show the process of inward transformation into an enlightening state of mind.

The Dalai Lama recited the rituals of the initiation and the various ceremonies connected with it in a sing-song voice. Although he spoke in the Central Tibetan dialect, pilgrims from other Himalayan countries seemed to be able to follow. The important points of the *Wang* were translated each evening to Western pilgrims by an English-speaking monk. But even those who had come unprepared and strictly as spectators could not help but feel the special radiance and solemnity of the occasion. Merely to watch His Holiness, to see the pilgrims' faces, and to walk around the ancient shrines was a religious experience for Buddhists and non-Buddhists alike. When, on the eighth day, the *Wang* ended and the pilgrims formed into a long single file to pay their respects to the Dalai Lama, we quietly joined in.

The Kalachakra Initiation

117 A *thanka* or scroll painting depicting the patron deity of the Kalachakra Initiation. This *thanka* was painted especially for the occasion by Tibetan painters in Dharamsala and served, together with the mandala, as an important visual aid in meditation.

118 Mönpa tribesmen from the northeast frontier area wearing their traditional caps made from yaks' hair.

119 Pilgrims milling around the tentlike structure where the Kalachakra Initiation was to take place. It contains the *thanka* and the mandala. In the background are two of the many shrines erected in this holy city of Buddhism by various countries.

120,121 Tibetan refugees and Mönpa pilgrams outside their tents in Bodhgaya.

122,123 Monk artists tracing the Kalachakra mandala with colored sand. This intricate design, a sort of cosmic diagram, also served as an aid in visualization and meditation throughout the initiation.

124 His Holiness the Dalai Lama giving the Kalachakra Initiation.

125 Pilgrims pay homage to His Holiness by tossing white scarves—*khatas* —towards his seat. In the foreground is the *sanga* or assembly of monks.

126 A group of Tibetan refugees during the initiation.

127 His Holiness the Dalai Lama surrounded by high lamas and dignitaries.

128 Tantric monks performing an ancient ritual dance during a rare esoteric form of meditation.

129 His Holiness the Dalai Lama officiating at the Kalachakra rites.

130,131,132 The symbolic opening of the wisdom eye and the "mandala mudra," or symbol of the universe. The latter is being formed with all ten fingers by a small *tulku*, or reincarnate monk, and with a *trenwa*—Buddhist rosary—by an older monk.

133 An old Tibetan woman using her prayer wheel. Inside the cylinder is a scroll of paper bearing sacred mantras.

134 A young monk in deep meditation.

135,136 The *sanga*, or assembly of monks, praying under the sacred Bodhi Tree in Bodhgaya. The tree is said to be an offshoot of the legendary pipal tree under which the Lord Buddha found enlightenment.

137,138 Pilgrims walk clockwise around a fire and throw offerings into the flame during a purification ceremony.

139 A Tibetan woman attending the butter lamps outside the main temple.

140 Candles are being lighted by pilgrims along the wall surrounding the Mahabodhi Temple.

141 The Mahabodhi Temple, Temple of Great Enlightenment, holiest site of Buddhism, in Bodhgaya, India.

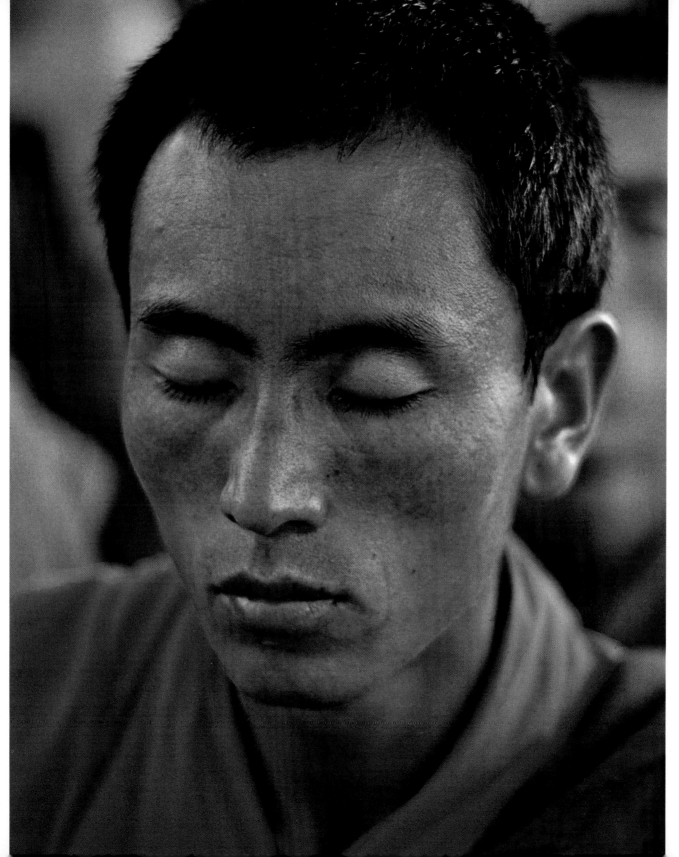